HAVE A GREAT DAY, ALWAYS!

SOMEDAY
in a place out west

by

jon sheppard

The Stevens Group

Published by:
The Stevens Group

Designed by:
Studio 202, 6 Jones Street, 5D, New York, NY 10014. 212-741-1610.

If there are errors in names, places, or things forgive the author.
P.O. Box 18101, Avon, CO. 81620-1801.

10 9 8 7 6 5 4 3 2 1

Library of Congress Catalog Card Number: 97-91781

Sheppard, J. 1942

Someday in a Place Out West

Photography

1. Non-Fiction - Authorship. 1. Title. II.
Title: Someday in a Place Out West.

ISBN 0-9658009-0-3

Printed and bound in Hong Kong.

Shrine Ridge, Mount of the Holy Cross   *Lupine*

Jon Sheppard's serendipitous tour of Colorado via photography, poetry, and prose is something to be savored slowly, like spending a warm September afternoon beside an alpine lake. With innocent, infectious enthusiasm, Jon invites us to join him on his discovery of the real Colorado. The fascinating places, people and anecdotes you'll encounter along the way will endear you long after you turn the last page.

Lyndon Lampert, Co-author, *A Climbing Guide to Colorado's Fourteeners*

In this beautifully illustrated book, Jon Sheppard has not only shown us the extraordinary beauty of Colorado, but his personal comments make interesting and exciting reading. His "odyssey of adventure" should not only warm the soul, but also challenge the heart of the sedentary individual. The Lord has provided us with great opportunities that we ignore, and hopefully this book will change all of us to take the time to explore our environment more closely, and revel in His masterpiece.

Dr. Kenneth Cooper, M.D., M.P.H., founder of the Cooper Clinic, Dallas, Texas

Upper Roaring Fork River

This book is dedicated to Kim Marie

Rifle Falls

Eastern Colorado

Saddle Rock, Eastern Plains

Acknowledgments

At the long insistence of friends and family to do this book on Colorado, I would like to thank: Jerry and Ruthie Millsaps for their loving guidance; Josh Millsaps for beating up his brand new four wheel drive pickup truck on all those bumpy back roads; Dale Clack for business advisement; Mary Bowman and Don Gore for their talent in correcting my grammar; Suzanne Venino, Tim and Cathy Hébert for technical editing; Joe Johnson, who is supposed to be retired but was kind enough to edit my stories and poems; Daryl Stevens for his many hours doing the layout and front cover design for me while I would sit and give lip service; Al Ansted for photographic and technical assistance; Scott Young, L'eau Vive Kayak Company; Broadacres Guest Ranch, Creede; Flattops Ranch, Toponas; Desert Rock Climbing Guides, Grand Junction; Jan Jones for her knowledge of Colorado National Monument; Don and Diana Barr, who offered a place to stay in Ouray; Jack and JJ Dilsrap of Branson, another place to stay; The Aspen Center for Environmental Studies, and Hallam Lake Nature Preserve, Aspen; Lissa Gilmour and her wonderful "wild" animals at Rocky Mountain Ark Wildlife Rehabilitation Center, Telluride; Dean Mershon and family for horse riding and back country trips, St. Mary's Glacier; Lyndon Lampert, co-author, *A Climbing Guide to Colorado's Fourteeners*, his guidance has kept me from being lost in the wilderness on many occasions. There are many others who have been of great help and assistance, and I do thank you too. A big thanks to the finest parents I could have asked for, they have stood by me through it all: Ken and Ruth Sheppard. And finally, I acknowledge the inspiration that has carried me, Jesus Christ.

Foreword

I have been photographing the Colorado landscape for more than twenty years and every step of the way — which I can tally in tens of thousands of driving, hiking, and rafting miles — has been a labor of love. Even when it means getting up in the dark at four in the morning to capture first light. Or carrying ninety pounds of camera equipment up a mountain. Or being marooned in my tent for days at a time during a raging, high country storm. The fact remains that I am out of doors, in the glory that is Colorado, doing what I love best. And I admire anyone who chooses to do the same.

Jon Sheppard has chosen this path. With camera in hand he has turned his eye to the mountains and flowers and fields. The years he has spent training his eye and refining his craft are evident in the pages of this book. Photography is an art form, but it is also a discipline, one that requires perserverance, hard work, time and energy. Jon makes the extra effort. He travels to remote places to put himself in the right place at the right time. Waiting for that perfect light, for the decisive moment—and knowing it when you see it—is as much a part of making good images as camera and film.

I am heartened to see how far Jon has come with his photography since we first met. Having encouraged him to pursue his art, I'm pleased to see that he now has a published book to exhibit his work, to share with others the Colorado that he sees. The stories, anecdotes, and poems he has written draw the viewer even further into his photography. I believe Jon has found his niche in the great outdoors and I look forward to seeing more of his books in the future.

John Fielder
Englewood, Colorado

Preface

I grew up with photography in my family. As we traveled we photographed the wonders of wherever we were. My first serious photographic journey was underwater photography in the Virgin Islands. In the years since then I have kept up with photography wherever my travels take me. A few years ago several friends insisted strongly that I to do a book on Colorado. With a slow start and many wrong turns, I have managed to assemble all this into a book. I have always enjoyed writing, and now it is all together.

Welcome to a thrilling odyssey of adventure; but beware: once you start this trip, there is no turning back. It will take you back in time to when you, too, dreamed of far-off exotic places, with strange and magical people, and unique moments of sharing. So hop on board. There is always room for one more. This book can be shared by all those who love the great outdoors, whether from the cushy softness of a big easy chair by a bright, crackling fire, or out on a windswept ridge leading to an obscure mountain top. With adventure in your heart and a jovial sense of humor, this will become an exciting challenge.

I will not have the opportunity to meet everyone who reads and enjoys this book. If by chance you catch me on a street corner by that old vacant five & dime store or down some whitewater canyon, let's have a cup of tea and share some good times together. Writing and photographing this has blessed me with tremendous gifts of happiness. It is a warm delight to present this to you.

When I was a small child growing up, Roy Rogers and John Wayne were my cowboy heroes. Their action-packed Westerns were thoroughly enjoyed because the good guys would always win. Some 40 years later, as I was traveling through the vast western mountains and valleys of Colorado, it was a warm surprise to relive those bygone days of yesteryear. I vividly visualized the cowboys and Indians, cattle rustlers and buffalo, the dusty roundups, and the chuck wagon next to a blazing campfire with tired, but happy cowboys having hot coffee, eating grub and telling wild stories of long ago.

The San Juans near Telluride

The photographs in this book were taken throughout Colorado. From the immense plains that cover the eastern third of the state, to the winding, barren mountains that zigzag the Continental Divide, to the sprawling open valleys of the central and western regions, it's all gorgeous and colorful Colorado. It has been a glorious joy to travel all of it. I remember those long, lonely, dusty roads out in the middle of nowhere. Finding an abandoned ranch house and wondering who built it? How long ago? Why did they leave? I would explore ghost towns and mining camps that are all quiet and still, except for the often mournful moaning of the wind. I have waited for hours for that special light to make a perfect picture, finding that sometimes it never would be. I have often gotten up long before daylight and driven 150 miles or more, or hiked and stumbled up a steep mountain trail just to catch the first morning rays of the sun. I would watch the land change, not only through the days but from season to season.

Imagine yourself traveling with me from the snow-covered mountains where winter is still king, down to the Front Range where there is bright, happy sunshine. The birds are singing, the grass fresh and green, the flowers are sprouting their petals. People are playing golf or tennis, running in shorts in the park, or having a picnic by a mirror-still lake.

It's nice to know that everywhere you go there is life.

Painted Daisy

Fall colors near Kebler Pass

The Gore Range

The Stop

Destiny awaits us unexpectedly, sometimes delightfully, and Colorado has more of this magic than most places I have been. As I was driving near Creede one day, I passed a ranch with horses for rent, and a little voice whispered to me, "Jon, you'd better stop!" I thought, "Naw, that's OK, I'll be back this way later." Four hours later I was passing by the ranch again and that little voice spoke to me with extreme urgency, "Jon, you'd really better stop!" I did a fast U-turn in the middle of the road, drove back, and pulled into the ranch. As I got out of my car I was greeted by a wonderful lady, owner Bea Collerette. I introduced myself and told her I was doing a photography book on Colorado, asking if it would it be possible to do a cowboy and horse shot here. She answered with a very enthusiastic, "Yes, I would love to have you take some pictures here!" I told her what I needed for the shoot. She replied, "Oh, I have just the person for you, and today is his birthday." She went over to the corral and talked to one of the young cowboys. He walked over to the bunkhouse to change into something for the pictures, and then came back to where she and I were standing. I introduced myself to him, "Hi, I'm Jon Sheppard." And he answered, "Hello, my name is Tom Mix." His great uncle was Tom Mix, cowboy movie star of the 1930s and 1940s.

I climbed a big hill that was covered in green
The top of that hill could seldom be seen
When I reached the top of that giant steep hill
My heart lifted up and my spirit was thrilled
To view the valley, so deep and so wide
Was a joy and a blessing of beauty and life
The river that flowed through the trees far below
Was crystal and clear from the melt of the snow
The mountains that stood on horizon beyond
Did sparkle with snow from the light of the sun
An eagle soared up, way high in the sky
He circled and glided with feelings of pride
He knows what it is to be happy and free
That free spirit in him is also in me.

Tom Murphy

We camped along a ridge just below timberline. It had been a good but tiring hike in to the high back country. The campfire snapped brightly with all the dry logs piled on it. Our tents were up, and we had just finished dinner as we sat and watched the red and yellow-orange coals glowing in the fire. We talked about the old miners' camps all through the area from a hundred years before, and how the miners hacked out trails to nowhere in search of silver and gold.

A loud snap cracked as someone stepped out of the darkness. "Howdy," he said. "Mind if I sit and rest a spell?" He looked like one of those guys you'd see in old photographs taken way back when. His clothes were dirty, as if he'd just emerged from a mine. I asked how he was doing and if he would like something to eat. "No thanks, I just like that nice warm fire." He was quite humble and happy to merely sit and talk to someone. Then he mused, "That fire reminds me of way back home." We continued to talk awhile, and then he said, "Well, I guess it's time to be a headin' on. I thank ya' for the company." Then he disappeared into the darkness. "Who was that?" asked my young friend Mike, from Georgia, in an excited voice! "Why, you don't know? That was ol' Tom Murphy," I said, "a miner of long ago who came out here from Tennessee. He was killed in a mine blast, but they say he saved a bunch of others before it caved in on him. He shows up around here every now and then just to sit by a fire, get warm, and have a chat with someone. It's quite a treat for him to come and visit."

And off through the valley in the pale moonlight
You could hear him singin' as he said, "Good night."

The Monument

Welcome to Western Colorado! The big town is Grand Junction, along the broad flowing Colorado River. Grand Junction is an up and coming area that grows by the day. Of the many attractions in the area, the BIG ONE is the Colorado National Monument. The great part about this unusual piece of real estate is that it seems more like a suburb west of town. No high mountain passes to climb. A fine paved road runs through it. You can stay in first class lodgings in Grand Junction or camp at the Monument. No scorching deserts. Yes, it is hot in the summer. This is the start of the great Southwestern canyons and deserts. Crowds can be heavy on the weekends in the summer, so plan your trip accordingly. And, the Monument itself is a unique place to visit.

Driving is the quickest and most convenient way to access the area. Rim Rock Drive will take you 23 miles along the edge of the canyon with many scenic overlooks. The Visitor Center and Monument Headquarters are "must" stops to visit and quite educational. Read some of the journal entries of those who have hiked and climbed here. John Otto pioneered the preservation of the area and wanted to make it a national park. In 1911 he succeeded and it became a national monument. During the exploratory time he managed to marry Beatrice Farnham, an artist from New England, and brought her to this remote and primitive area to "enjoy" the land. The honeymoon and wilderness lodging consisted of a large tent. I believe she lasted about four months, got smart, and said, "So long, farewell, adios."

If you take the time, and properly prepare yourself, the many trails that abound throughout the monument are wonderfully rewarding. Many of the Grand Junction locals hike the two miles of Serpent's Trail. It follows the old access road at the east end of the Monument. Some run, some walk, it's a 1500 foot elevation change that takes about two and a half hours. The trails in the Monument are anywhere from a few hundred yards to fourteen miles round trip. You will witness many unusual rock formations, from the massive rounded Coke Ovens, to Window Rock, Devils Kitchen, and many more. It is also possible to find petroglyphs left long ago by Native Americans who inhabited the area. There are fossil remains of shellfish and dinosaurs.

Colorado National Monument

Choosing the right time is important for the perfect picture. Late March, April, and May normally bring the best desert flowers; it won't be too warm. Likewise, summer is quite hot; carry lots of water if you travel then. September and the fall offer the desert's version of vibrant fall colors. In the winter, when there is good snow fall, Liberty Cap Trail is excellent for cross-country skiing. The trail is fourteen miles round trip, and it is uphill coming back. It is possible to find many scenic overlooks along the rim of the canyon. For early risers, watch the enchantment of the sunrise lighting, and at sunset watch as the evening light turns the rock formations into a warmth of soft gold.

There's a pot o' gold at the end of a rainbow
I found it there, it's true!
But the gold I found was from my heart
It was a thought of you.

San Luis Valley

Gray Wolf

An Indian massacre happened a long time ago. It was a cold and bitter winter. The snow had been unusually deep, and there was precious little game that year. When the bad men came into camp, they left no survivors on that frigid, sunless day. They say the coyotes howled all night long from the loss of all their friends.

Now on this starry, full-moon evening, I listened to the slow, reverberating beat of the Indian drums and watched the dancing shadows moving slowly around a bright, flashing fire. The spirits were chanting mystical words I could not understand. Just as the sun went down, I looked up on a ridge above the trees and saw the spirit of Gray Wolf as he cried for all his people.

Then all was very quiet in the gentle breeze that night
And sleep I did not conquer, till the pale of morning light.

Mt. Sopris

An eagle flew over the mountain today
The first one I'd seen since I'd been away
He gave a sharp cry to welcome me home
To a place where the deer and the bobcat roam
For I've traveled far places on land and on sea
The adventures I've had would last lifetimes for me
From the Amazon to Alaska to lands time forgot
To the strange and the mystic of things that were not
With the sun and the moon and the stars in the sky
Made it great to be home, to be free and alive
It was just like a dream, the years rolled away
All the things I had lost, and those that were saved
But the one thing I've learned, and the last that I'll say
There will always be a tomorrow . . . because there is today.

Branson, Colorado

Elevation: 6,298 feet. Population: 63. Almost in the middle of nowhere sits the quiet but warm, little community of Branson. It is about fifty miles east of Trinidad and only a mile or so north of the New Mexico state line. Branson was once a bustling railroad town. Now, quieter times prevail.

Jack Dilsrap was born here. His granddad homesteaded 20,000 acres back in 1905. He and I planned a hike up to Saddle Rock for a magnificent view of the Great Eastern Plains. We hopped into his dusty, rusty old pickup and off through a couple of cattle pastures we drove. He parked on the side of the mesa among ponderosa pines, and as we hiked an old access road, he asked me if I was allergic to poison ivy or scared of snakes. I answered, "No!" and off we went into the bright, early evening sun.

The trail climbed among the trees to a low saddle that dropped off hundreds of feet to the west. To our right was a wall of solid rock. We scrambled out on a ledge about thirty feet above the ground, where someone had hung a fat rope to climb to the top. With careful moves — Jack first, the camera gear, and then me — we were on the top. It was flat and smaller than a football field. The Spanish Peaks and the Sangre de Cristo Range were to the west. To the northwest we could see the shadowy outline of Pikes Peak. To the east were the great plains of Colorado and New Mexico. I shot the setting sun, then walked over to the other side, sat and waited thirty minutes for the moon to come up from the east. Then, I shot that too.

The climb down wasn't any easier. The trail was half lit by the moon and we had to watch where the water from the springs ran across the trail. I never did catch poison ivy and didn't step on a snake either.

The sunset was a brilliant red, as it faded into night
Homes were still, snug and warm, as I turned off one last light.

Spanish Peaks

Cowboys and Ranches

"Go West young man, go West," said Horace Greeley. So many did. They came by horseback, covered wagon, train, and some even walked. That is how it started. First the explorers, trappers, and adventure seekers looking for silver and gold. Then came the families, who brought togetherness and permanence. From these families came the growing towns and the sprawling ranches of the West. From these ranches came the cowboys. I don't know exactly where they began, but here is where they are.

Up long before sunrise, they are chasing cattle, mending a fence, bailing hay, or fixing a broken down pickup truck. And when the sun has gone down, they are still at it. Through the cold blast of winter in knee deep snow, to the scorching heat of summer, they are there. The wind often blowing, the cowboy is always on the move. His face is weather worn and deeply suntanned. His hands are calloused and rough, but there is a magic twinkle in his deep-set eyes. You can see a gentle smile across his face, his firm handshake gives a warm welcome. He is happy with his work and where he is. His best companion is his horse, always trusted and dependable.

I had the enjoyable experience of following them one day on a cattle move. I found rancher and veterinarian Kirk Shiner and crew herding about 1500 cattle from various fields to a central location. A casual lunch break turned into a quick free-for-all when the cattle didn't understand just what a lunch break was supposed to be. They started walking through an opening in the fence and on down the road. Not only did they wander down the road, but into other fields, that for some reason, were left open. "It's round up time again!" Ahead of the grand parade, I was able to capture the Western ambiance. Under control, and a few miles down the road, they were moved to another grazing area. With the cowboys and cowgirl, Wrangler the wonder dog, the cattle, and wide open ranges, this was a great day of adventure. At last all of the cattle were in, the gate was closed and a long deserved break was at hand. Finally, late in the warm October sun, lunch.

I would suppose that is why "the cowboy" is such an enduring legend, and why so many stories, songs, and movies have been made about him. Admired and loved by all, he is a one-of-a-kind, never to be found anywhere else. Often imitated, but never duplicated . . . the American cowboy.

Red Mountain Pass

Summer Mountains

Colorado is breathtaking, especially if you drive from sea level to 14,000 foot Mt. Evans or Pikes Peak. Go at sunrise or sunset when the light gently colors the landscape. Note the different life zones as you drive higher. Traveling from green grass and hardwood trees to bristlecone pines and alpine tundra you will find barren rock at the highest summit. While you are at it, look for some ski tracks down a lingering snow chute. Watch for the curious mountain goats. Listen for the high-pitched yelp of marmots or the tiny pikas that whistle your intrusion. The weather can change at a moment's notice; be prepared for sunshine, hail, snow, rain, strong winds, thunder and lightning. Life abounds here. Take the time to see it.

Grays Peak

Wet Mountain Valley

Mount of the Holy Cross

Piney Lake and the Gore Range Mountains

Shrine Pass

The old homestead looks a bit run down, and the fence is sagging too
The trees are turning, the days are short
And my thoughts are still of you.

Flat Top Wilderness

The Big Wall

The trail grew narrow and steep. We had passed through the forest far below, and the towering evergreen trees seemed tiny now that we stood high above them. Rocks and boulders covered the barren ground. Patches of exquisitely delicate alpine wildflowers, lichens, and mosses were the only plants growing at this elevation. As we climbed through the boulder field, an occasional pika would give a high whistle of alarm. Although the sun shone brightly, it seemed quite cool. A light breeze rambled in from somewhere else. Panting with each step in the ultra-thin atmosphere, we slowly climbed onward. Rounding a sharp bend, there it was — a sheer wall of rock that stretched upward for what seemed like forever into a cloudy mist at the top.

Uncompahgre Peak

Finding a large, flat spot, we stopped for the day and made camp. It was cold but the clearest night I had ever seen, with countless brilliant stars in the sky. Before we knew it, there was a pale glow of light forming from the east. It turned into a rosy red dawn, and a clear day to climb. Up one long crack system using chocks and runners for protection, I counted seven pitches before we came up under a giant overhanging roof. We made a traverse on a frightfully thin ledge to the left, and found an open-face route to the top. Small hand and footholds with excellent protection placements made the climb exhilarating.

Then all of a sudden, there was no place to climb. We were on the summit! We sat, caught our breath, and inhaled all that was around us. The far-distant mountain ranges to the west gave way to an immense basin to the south with more mountains trailing farther beyond. On the backside we could see a small herd of mountain goats far below, bright white and shiny in the midday sun. A cold wind blew in, signaling to us that it was time to descend. The back trail was mighty steep, and snow patches still covered spots along the route. We reached camp just before dusk, with the purple-red rays of the setting sun saying good night to some tired friends.

Ouray

Vail

Colorado City at Fairplay

Towns

Within the borders of Colorado there are all kinds of towns. There are mountain towns, valley towns, rural towns far out on the plains, ghost towns, mining towns, ski towns, and even the highest incorporated town in North America — Leadville, 10,152 feet above sea level. Most of these towns have a Chamber of Commerce or visitor center to help you get to know the area. And a few even have historical centers to visit.

Silverton

Mountain Majesty

Leaving their home in Virginia, the Johnson family slowly worked their way West by horsedrawn wagon. They stopped here and there en route, doing odd jobs and temporary work, so they could reach the place they had dreamed about for years. It's a place with high, snow-covered mountains and deep river valleys covered with green. It would have lands for pasturing cattle and rich soil to grow crops. As they continued on their journey West, the land seemed like an endless sea of rolling flatlands with small farms, wooded countrysides, and flowing rivers. With little money, the family knew that despair was always close by, but onward they moved. Through stormy weather and the scorching heat of summer, day after day they kept following the westward sun.

Each morning they would arise long before dawn to start their daily trek. One day, as the first pale streaks of morning light started to filter through the clouds high above, one of the girls, Marsha, saw something excitingly strange on the horizon far ahead. She kept looking and looking but uttering not a word. As the sun slowly climbed higher, she saw an inspiring sight. With delight she cried out, "They're purple! Look everyone, they're purple! They're purple!" After she woke up the rest of the family, her older brother asked, "What's purple?" "The mountains!" she said. "They're purple! See?"

We chopped cotton in Alabama, picked beans in Tennessee.
We crossed the mighty Mississippi, it was wide, so very wide.
We chased wild pigs and turkeys in a place called Arkansas,
And when sweet Betsy died we buried her on a hillside facing east,
Where the rising sun would shine on her first thing in the morning.
Across Oklahoma, the land it rolled like an endless sea.
It was hot, windy, and cold. It changed from week to week.
There it was one morning, just as the sun came up,
A range of mountains stretching way across the horizon,
Filling our hearts with tears of joy.
The rising rays of the sun made the peaks shine in a beautiful, soft purple.

Boreas Pass

Hallam Lake Nature Preserve

Most people think of Aspen for its great skiing, glitzy night life, and homes of the superstars. There is one part of Aspen that everyone rich or poor should be sure to visit. It's the nature preserve at Hallam Lake. During the winter they offer snowshoe tours around the lake and on the surrounding mountains. Year round they have guided walks and talks, as well as birds of prey, ecology, and environmental programs to help educate all who come for a visit. Pictured here is Rick Lofaro with his friend, "Mr. Owl," and Brian Flynn with good ol' "Mr. Eagle." You will enjoy their warm and courteous hospitality should you wander into the Hallam Lake Nature Preserve.

Hike a Trail

The trail starts where the road ends — unless the car stops earlier — then, just add that much more distance. Evergreen trees stretch all around, with stands of aspens here and there. The trail kicks up a steep, winding curve, with rocks and old tree limbs scattered along the way. The noise of tumbling water almost jumps out at me as I make a sharp turn in the trail. It's a struggle to make my way through the dense foliage to the cascading water. I watch it with fascination as it crashes around the boulders scattered all about. The old logs and rocks in the river are covered with moss.

I head back to the trail, passing the fallen-down remains of an old trapper's cabin. There's not much left of it now. I come upon a high mountain meadow, filled with flowers, shrubs, old tree stumps, and decaying logs. There are lupine, columbine, Indian paintbrush, shooting star, and many more. Oh look! A marmot is eating his summer's fill. The trail winds steeper, climbing above the tree line. There the grass gives way to lichen and moss on the rocks. Then the trail sort of fades into the scree slope that climbs up and out of sight. Somewhere way up there, along with a snowfield or two, is the cold, windy summit. Good Luck!

San Juan Mountains

Mountain stream La Plata Peak Trail

San Juan Mountains

Arkansas River Mt. Elbert

There's a river that flows from mountains to sea
And it beckons for all, to come follow me
For many are chosen but few only come
From the frozen far north to the tropical sun
From icy blue summits of snowcapped peaks
The snowmelt does trickle, it gurgles and speaks
Through granite rock canyons it crashes on down
By dropping and splashing it plays like a clown
It brings life to lowlands and valleys beyond
To fields and green forests that sing its sweet song
Flowing silently on, past you and past me
It flows to its end, in the endless blue sea.

Nighttime

It's another lonely night off a dusty back road. The campfire is warm and casts fleeting shadows through the early dusk of a setting sun. The moon is rising through the piñon pines. It's peaceful now, with a cool, gentle breeze coming in from the west. Off in the distance, high up on a hill, a coyote gives a piercing cry as a pair of ravens are heading home. Then slowly, a velvety curtain of black covers the sky with a million sparkling stars scattered from one end to the other. The day is done, and it's time for a rest.

Alpine Daisy

Flowers

Wherever you go in Colorado, you will always find flowers, from the sweeping plains, to the foothills, to the flanks of 14,000-foot mountains. Some, like sunflowers, grow taller than a man. Others, such as the alpine wildflowers found at the highest elevations, are so small it is difficult to understand how they survive at all.

I do not pretend to know anything about flowers. I just photograph them, because they are beautiful, and they don't run away when I approach them.

Blanket Flower

Fairy Trumpet

Alpine Daisy

Indian Paintbrush

Flat Tops Wilderness

With the deep blue sky, warm days, and cold nights come the changing of the leaves. Fall is at its fullest. Brilliant colors flash everywhere. The elk and deer are on the move.

Soon, there will be the silence of winter white.

Upper Roaring Fork River

The Rivers

Colorado is the birthplace of three mighty rivers: the Arkansas, the Rio Grande, and the Colorado. They ramble and meander to the farthest reaches of America. I would like to share with you some interesting views of the Arkansas and Colorado Rivers.

The Arkansas starts high above Leadville, Colorado, just south of Fremont Pass and the Continental Divide. Directly behind this photo is where the headwaters begin. You could possibly step across here, but you'd probably fall into rather deeeeeep drifts of snow.

Wild sections of the river tumble rapidly down the Arkansas Valley. They have become famous for whitewater rafting, kayaking, and canoeing. The river carved this scenic valley and is surrounded by fourteen mountains over 14,000 feet high, with many of them rising 6,000 feet above the valley floor.

Here is Scott Young casually "cruising" on Lake Creek just above Twin Lakes. He is a fellow Tennessean who runs his own kayak business here in Colorado. Lake Creek, which flows into Twin Lakes, is a major tributary of the Arkansas. It begins near 12,095 foot Independence Pass on the Continental Divide.

As the Arkansas empties onto the Great Eastern Plains, it supplies water to millions of people while en route to the Mississippi River which is approximately 1,102 river miles down the road from the Colorado-Kansas state line.

A mighty river the Colorado! Starting on the western side of Rocky Mountain National Park, it curves its way southwest, meeting the Eagle River at an intriguing point call Dotsero. The town was named Dot-zero because that is where the railroad started building both eastward and westward. The river turns almost due west at this point and has carved a miniature Grand Canyon east of Glenwood Springs, making for a beautiful drive along Interstate 70. Take time and hike up to the mysterious and enchanting Hanging Lake, or even try whitewater rafting through Glenwood Canyon. Then, go for a relaxing soak in the Glenwood Hot Springs pool.

The next we see of the Colorado, it has grown into a broad, flat river at Grand Junction. Here it joins the Gunnison River. As it flows west toward the Utah state line it enters Ruby and Horsethief Canyons. In the late spring of 1993 the river peaked out at about 42,000 cubic feet per second, creating an amazing summer of river running. My friend Rick Smith rafted seventeen miles of Westwater Canyon in Utah in only two and one half hours. That's fast!

Upper Colorado

Surf Colorado

Mt. Sopris

Colors

As summer yields to autumn, the magic of fall colors in the Rocky Mountains is an unforgettable sight. The shortening of the days and cooling of the nights cause a profound change in the land. Starting early in the high country, the exquisite changing of the leaves works its magic for all to enjoy. When you travel here, there is something special about the different moods. The early morning light, or the warm, soft evening glow — it's a wonderful glory that brings out all the splendor of colors. The fall sky has that special brilliance of deep blue that you can only visualize and feel in your heart.

Driving by car you can reach many locations in just a few minutes, or an hour or two. Hike a trail carpeted in fallen leaves and you will be in your own world of back country beauty. Take the time to walk along a gurgling stream. Watch the cascading water bounce down and around the moss-covered boulders in a wonderful mountain setting. If you enjoy trout fishing, go for it! They are big and fat from the summer feeding. Catch and release those beauties or have a fabulous trout dinner with melted butter. Please, don't forget your fishing license!

Enjoy a quiet picnic by a mirror-still lake, or sit by a thundering waterfall, and listen to your heart beat. I hope that you are traveling with friends, family or someone special with whom to share this. Explore the old log cabins, long abandoned and slowly falling away. View them through the golden yellow leaves. You wonder, who built them? How long ago? When you visit a ghost town, listen for the rapping of the wind, or is it a mystic voice from the distant past? If you are fortunate, you may see some elk or deer in a wide open meadow. Start out early in the morning or look for them late in the evening. Listen for the bugle of the elk . . . it sounds more like a French horn than an elk.

When you are up on a high ridge overlooking a far distant valley, enjoy the spectacular views. Along with the dramatic fall colors, watch for a soaring eagle or other birds of prey. They are catching the thermals rising off the valley floor, searching for their next meal. If you are camping, listen to the coyotes howl at night. It's a sound you will never forget. And, after a long day of fun and excitement, enjoy the deep red rays of the setting sun. Then watch the countless number of stars in the sky as the blackness of night falls all around you.

Hanging Lake in Glenwood Canyon

Kebler Pass

Upper Crystal River

Youth

Ponce de Leon was on the right track, but never got there. You see, I've discovered that the fountain of youth is not a place, or an elixir, but an attitude from within. Simply look at a retired school teacher, factory worker, or professional person who now spends time teaching skiing, climbing mountains, running rivers, or taking casual walks through the high country, enjoying all that God has given us. I know; I'm one of them. That is, I was once young, but I'll never grow old. There will always be that childlike quality in me. Maturity, yes. Responsibilities, yes. Youthful, always. I am a participant, not just an observer.

Rodeo Cowboys

Rodeo cowboys ride the circuit every season. Taking off from work, they head out to the rodeos, traveling half the night pulling a horse trailer, staying in an economy motel or camping out, paying their entry fee, and maybe lasting two seconds on a bronco or bull. If they are lucky, they go home without any broken parts. If by chance they win, and someone always does, they will have a few hundred dollars to buy some gas and food till the next rodeo.

Rodeo clowns are always funny and great entertainment. They make a good show, but most important, they are an essential safety source for the cowboys. They put themselves between the bull and the riders, and at times take some bone jarring hits. The fast-paced action the cowboys create, from calf roping to the bucking big animals, will make a memorable rodeo experience for the entire family. And, it can really get wild if a bull jumps a fence!

The angel of the Lord struck his sword across the sky
It lit the cosmic universe like a flash before my eye
The demons were all scattered, defeated and forlorn
For another soul was salvaged and saved by our great Lord.
The road to win was rocky and covered with traps and snares
The travel hard and treacherous, dark valleys everywhere
And then the sun shone brightly, the clouds did all break free
He touched the heart of the one I love, this was for you and me.

Home

One day I stood on a high, rocky ridge above the trees. It was so clear that I could see for many miles in every direction. The valleys far below were green and teeming with life. There were businesses, shops, schools, and ranches. As evening approached, the golden rays of the setting sun cast long, dark shadows. Down below, the workday over, people would be heading home. They would be going to a place filled with pictures of family on the walls and antiques passed on from those before. There, that special someone would be waiting at the door to reach out and say, "I love you." I'm home!

Mt. Sopris

The days are getting longer now, the sun is rising high
The chipmunks on a fallen log are running swiftly by
The flowers blooming on the hills form a giant colored sea
The clouds across the jagged peaks say, "Come and follow me!"

Wet Mountain Valley

Sand Dunes

The Great Sand Dunes National Monument is a most fascinating natural wonder. You can first see the dunes from many miles away, and the closer you get the bigger they grow. Sand blowing across the San Luis Valley for millions of years from the far off San Juan's, has caused a major pileup against the Sangre de Cristo Range.

Most people enjoy the view from the Visitor Center or take short hikes across Medano Creek. Be sure to bring your camera and a heavy duty garbage bag. To slide down the dunes, find a steep section, step into your garbage bag, and down you go! The sand is mighty warm in the summer, so wear some old tennis shoes. To cool off, just wade in the snow-melted waters of Medano Creek. For those with four wheel drive vehicles, head up the eastern side of the Dunes to explore. It's amazing that most people see just one or two percent of the Dunes.

Crystal River

In their heart everyone "sees" in black and white, but there are a very few who "see" in a color so vivid, so deep, so rich, and so different. You'll know it when that one special time in your life — maybe, only once in your lifetime — it happens to you. But when it does, it will touch you deeper than the bottom of the sea, higher than the highest mountain, more quietly than a falling feather — but forever, it will be!

White River National Forest

San Luis Valley

Deserts

Not to be outdone by the majestic mountains are the ever-changing, enchanting deserts of Colorado. There is something unique and mysterious about the vast emptiness of a desert. Cruise a back road and see what I mean.

Mining Days of Long Ago

Somewhere along here many years ago there was a mine cave-in with the loss of a number of lives. They never reopened that place. But sometimes, if you're lucky, when the air is still and the moon is full and bright, you may hear the faint hum of machinery or get a whiff of exploded dynamite. And you might even hear a voice or two singing miners' songs, or telling one another what they're going to get their kids for Christmas.

There was a tragic mine cave-in, and all in there were lost
Through sweat and dirt and grime and hell they paid the final cost
And though a rainbow crossed the sky into a setting sun
The families that were left behind would mourn for years to come.

The Glenwood Fire

In the summer of 1994 lightning struck just west of Glenwood Springs causing a forest fire, which burned over 2,000 acres. The biggest threat was to the part of town on the north side of the Colorado River. Between five and six hundred volunteers and professional fire fighters battled for about nine days to stop the raging fire. They were assisted by airplanes and helicopters dropping a million gallons of water and flame retardants. Fourteen fire fighters died trying to stop this blaze.

Fourteen of the very best, they gave their final all
To fight that raging monster, that blazing fiery ball
This tribute to their valor, the least that I can do
Commemorates their courage and honors now those few.

Another River in Time

I watched a crystal-clear stream as it crashed and splashed its way among the giant boulders. Dropping, turning, and washing back on itself, it created a churning rivulet. It was a road far less traveled than the back road I had just walked, and now many miles away.

The scene's captivating beauty was everywhere, from the high, craggy canyon walls filled with cracks running in smooth poetic lines, to the lone, high-gliding osprey soaring above it. As the river made an abrupt turn, it tumbled over a funnel-shaped rock and dropped into a pool of emerald-green water. Beneath a boulder-strewn wall was a beautiful, white sandy beach. As I gazed a little farther down the canyon, the walls slowly receded into gently rolling hills. The river of crystal emptied into the farmlands of another time and place.

Upper Roaring Fork River

Vail

As the setting sun sinks softly in the west, evening lights twinkle on throughout the valley. Another exhilarating day of winter fun is done. Now it's time for a quiet dinner with someone special.

Snow

When the mountains are covered in a smooth, fresh white blanket of snow, playing magic with the light, you have to be here to enjoy the view for yourself. Strap on some snowshoes, make cross-country tracks, schuss downhill, or simply stand quietly at the forest's edge and draw deep into your heart all the great outdoors.

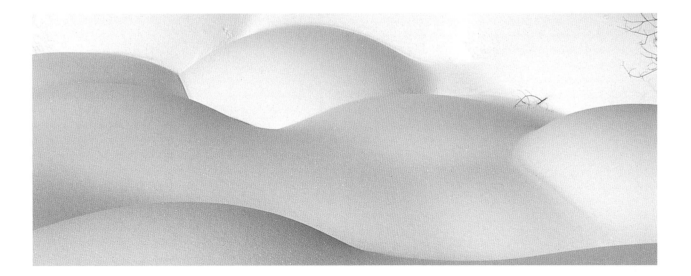

Ski Country

Colorado has some of the finest skiing in the world. There are ski resorts scattered from one end of the state to the other. I suppose I could do a whole book on the subject. But come out and try one for yourself, as I did just a few years ago. My very first ski day was at the Loveland Ski Area. Out of control and falling seemed to be a way of life in those long beginner days. The first season I didn't fall getting off the lift was a major breakthrough for me. Since then I've skied many miles and well over four million vertical feet, including eighteen ski resorts in one day! Now, it's all downhill from here!

China Bowl, Vail

Sun Down Bowl, Vail

Ski Colorado

Well, it's only a few hundred feet to the bottom!

Prima Cornice, Vail

The season is over and I'm all packed
I'm headed on home but I will be back
I skied the big bumps and jumped the steep chutes
The snow would explode up over my boots.

Through stormy weather and bitter, blue cold
The skiing was great and never got old
The sun is now out and shines bright today
The snow slowly melts and trickles away.

The birds sing sweetly, the grass is now green
The creeks in the vales, all gurgle and ring
It won't be too long till autumn will come
The trees will turn bright with shortening sun.

And then one crisp day the north winds will blow
And cover the steeps with new fallen snow
I'll then know it's time, back here once again
New faces to see and meet dear old friends.

It happened like that, one cold, winter night
The snow was untracked in the new morning light
Gliding in silence, straight down through the trees
The powder is deep, way over my knees!

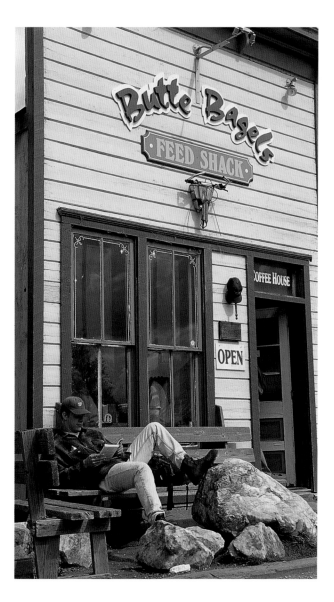

Beaver Creek

The Rocky Mountains

Formed many millions of years ago, the Rocky Mountains stretch far beyond the state boundaries of Colorado. But this is where I live, so this is where the story starts. My first view of them was driving west on I-70, somewhere east of Limon. Over a rise in the interstate, and there they were! I'll never forget that beautiful sight. It was mid March and the mountains were totally white with snow. The first I saw was Pikes Peak, far off in the distance. The closer I drove the larger they grew, stretching all across the horizon. Once past Denver, I was suddenly up on Genesee Mountain staring at snow covered St. Mary's Glacier along with other peaks all around her.

There are 54 peaks over 14,000 feet plus a few subpeaks thrown in. They are commonly know as "14ers." So come and join me in an enchanting and exciting trip around, between, and up on top of some of these colossal giants.

My first attempt was a "hike" up Grays and Torreys Peaks. It was mid October, and there was already a lot of snow on the ground. At about 13,000 feet I got sick enough to stop, but my girlfriend went on up through the clouds to the summit. Well, that was a start! Finally I bought *A Climbing Guide to Colorado's Fourteeners,* by Walter Borneman and Lyndon Lampert. I called Lyndon to thank him for a very informative guide. I got lost three times in a parking lot, then got out of my car! Seriously though, it is an excellent guide book.

One note of warning, please be well-prepared and understand what you are getting into. The roads, sometimes quite rough, will take you well up into the high country. The trailheads and parking areas are easy to find, but once you are on the trail you are on your own. Time and weather are of great concern. Know what you are climbing and your physical limitations. Remember, there is always another day. These giants were here long before us and they will still be here long after we are gone. Oh yes, you don't conquer a mountain, it lets you share its presence. Please treat them all with great respect. Pack it in, pack it out.

Mt. Princeton

I try to start a climb as the pale streaks of light are breaking to the east. Usually the trail will start somewhere below timberline. After awhile, as the warming rays of the sun shine through, I will suddenly find myself walking and panting into a wide open meadow, gasping in the ultra-thin atmosphere. I have yet to find someone to carry me up, especially at a zero budget with no tip.

In the meadows, enjoy the wildflowers that abound all around. You will find shooting star, columbine, Indian paintbrush, and lupine, just to name a few. The flowers are not only beautiful to photograph, but there are so many to chose from. Also watch for the marmots eating all they can. After the flowers comes a variety of rocks, lichens, sand, dirt and more rocks. Listen and look for the squeaky little pika. About the size of a large mouse, they whistle with alarm at your intrusion.

Oops! The trail seems to have disappeared. All you have to do is keep going up, or so it would seem. Search wisely, it is there. Please be watchful of the loose rocks. Some are the size of a large truck and when you step or jump onto them, they may start to tilt or roll. If they are around, look for the the mountain goats that inhabit the area. They are just as curious about you as you are of them.

I haven't even mentioned the awesome views as you climb higher. Many times you will see other 14ers right next to you, or seventy miles away. Here you are at 12,000, 13,000, 13,500 feet above sea level. Would you believe 99% of all the land in North America is now below you? The oxygen in the atmosphere has dropped to about one half of what it is at sea level.

Stressed and tired, onward I would climb. Then, all of a sudden, what land that is left around me seems to narrow down and level off. There is an eeriness to all that wide open space. I'm on the summit! Rejoice! I made it! Finally, a real rest. Time to get more food energy back into my system. Some of the summits are the size of the flight deck of an aircraft carrier . . . others the size of a rather large living room. Don't forget to sign the summit register, and take lots of pictures. The many views are totally awe inspiring. Got a cell phone? Call your family back home in Ohio. Collect! Sometimes I might be on the top for an hour. It all depends on the weather. Lightning is lethal, but that is another very interesting story. Well from here all we have to do is climb back down the mountain. Yeah, it's easy on your lungs but will kill your legs. Gee, if I just had someone to carry me, or at least my pack. Oh Jerry!

Missouri Lakes Trail

Grays Peak

From Mt. Sneffels, San Juan Mountains

I climbed a thousand mountains in a moment's pause in time
I saw a million sunsets in the thickness of a dime
I crossed an unknown galaxy, so very far above
And traveled on to secret worlds, so I could bring you love.
I saw a giant rainbow, stretch all across the sky
The colors flooded everywhere, and glittered in my eye
I flew across the vast beyond, through places far and near
And felt your warm and loving touch, so very close and dear.

I hiked an ancient valley in a land of long ago
I saw the magic mountains all covered white with snow
The stream was pure as crystal as it bounced around a bend
I almost lost your image, but then you came back again
Your eyes were shining brightly, and a lovely, clean, clear blue
I touched your face and we embraced, my love is all for you.

Alpenglow   *Historic Camp Hale*

Time Together

Maybe you know how it is when, just once in your life, you meet that one very special person, but it may not be the perfect time. Then one day, the long winter snows melt. The creeks start to gurgle. The birds start to sing. Flowers begin to bloom and there's the music of life in the air. You just know that God cares, and there shall be two together — not one alone.

In all the world I've traveled, to seek out what is fine
And one thing I discovered is . . .
Paradise is not a place, but wonderful state of mind.

The Spire

John Otto was the pioneering founder of Colorado National Monument. He first climbed Independence Monument in 1910. Drilling holes in the rock, John hammered two-inch lead pipes to use as a climbing ladder. He also carved out handholds and footholds along the way. Two years later John climbed it again and raised the U.S. flag to celebrate the Fourth of July. According to Monument officials, the pipes were removed in the 1950s because they were becoming loose and dangerous. Eighty years after John Otto made his first climb, three Grand Junction climbers repeated it, scaling the the giant monolith and raising Old Glory on July 4, 1990.

I had the privilege of climbing Independence Monument with K.C. Baum, Bob Fisher, and Rick Smith of Desert Rock Guides. We climbed it one hot summer day in 1993. They moved over the rock just like the fast-moving lizards that live there. For me it was an ever-enduring struggle — breathless and semi-dehydrated every foot of the way. The climb was more than worth it, though, as the view from the top was spectacular. People at the overlook on Ridge Road Drive cheered when we raised the flag. A few rappels, down climb, another rappel or two and we were back at the bottom of that great spire. Hot and tired, I hiked out with the rest, showered, and crashed for a three-hour nap. You know, I still don't understand why the Jeep wasn't there! Climb it again? Someday!

Independence Monument

The birds had all sheltered, it's the end of the day
The deer at the river and the cows eating hay
We lit a small fire that crackled and popped
The moon was just rising and the wind had just stopped
And over a hill on a ridge out of sight
Came the howl of coyotes in the pale evening light.

The sandy roads I've traveled, I've left so far behind
To seek my fame and fortune in another place and time
The asphalt streets of Broadway glittered not with gold
The hustle of the city, when it got so very old
Just one more river crossing, and one more hill to climb
I'll see that magic valley so deep inside my mind
And then one day I'll cross it, and peace then I will find.

Yampa River

Snow Snakes

Have you ever heard about the legendary snow snakes? Elusive creatures, they lurk just below the surface of the snow and are notorious for tripping unsuspecting skiers. The chances of actually seeing one are maybe one in a million. It would surely be a lifetime event.

One lucky day I not only found one, but it was sleeping in a tree! There had been a vicious blizzard all night long, and I was out early to photograph the scenic wonders of the mountains. I quickly took its picture before it noticed someone was near.

But you know what? As the sun slowly rose higher and the warming rays touched all around, he seemed to fade into a far off distant memory. I would surmise that he will be back again on another snowy day, somewhere up in the high country.

The Gore Range

Moonlight

When the moon is full and bright out here you don't need a flashlight to see where you're going. You just keep walking till you trip, stumble, or fall into something.

This photograph is the startling, ever-awesome, fantastically wonderful, Black Canyon of the Gunnison River. I shot this at night. But wait a few minutes, the moon will be up and then you can see even more!

I took a walk the other day, not knowing where to stop
And when I stood and looked around, I was at the very top
The trek seemed long, as I traveled on, but peace it brought to me
It was so nice to see so far, the feeling set me free!

South Park

All I ever wanted was just someone to love
A special gift from heaven sent by God above
To share good times together with joy and happiness
Or when we slip and stumble . . .

Dwellings

Old cabins are quaint and picturesque. Whenever I photograph them I feel a sense of the past. I am inspired by the history written into that old wood grain, and I let my imagination carry me back to those days of long ago. It makes me think of another time in the growth of our country. How did they survive those early years? How did they raise cattle, grow crops, endure the harsh winters? Can you hear the children playing? The dogs barking? The sound of horses running? The cattle calling off in the distance? I can still smell the hot baked apple cobbler cooling on the open kitchen window sill. Out in the fields I can smell the freshly cut hay, and the sweet smell of impending evening showers.

Creede

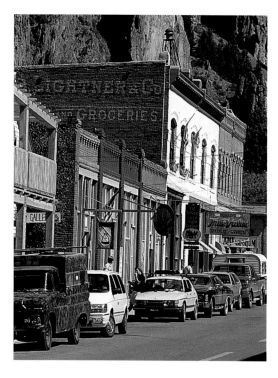

The town of Creede has certainly found its place in history books. It was once a booming mining town with the distinction of having some of the richest silver ore to be found. It also has the distinction of being the locale of the shooting of Bob Ford by Edward Kelly. Bob, who had shot and killed Jesse James back in St. Joseph, Missouri, came West and opened a tent saloon. Edward Kelly, seeking revenge for the death of Jesse James, killed Bob Ford. No one knows where Bob Ford is buried. As for Ed, he did his time in the state prison. I'm surprised he wasn't hanged then and there back in Creede. The town has suffered its share of devastating fires and floods, and the cemetery still stands from the roaring days of old. Both night and day Creede was a wild, hell-raising town.

The Rio Grande Valley, what a most gorgeous place to visit! Starting high on the Continental Divide, the river winds its way down through the wide open country of Mineral County. Fishing is great wherever you stop to throw in a line. Here in the high country, you can see much of it on State Route 149, the Silver Thread Highway. The valley is filled with history, well-appointed ranches, and play spots.

Rio Grande near Creede

Rocky Mountain Wildlife

Lissa Gilmour has a long history of family in Colorado. One of her ancestors was an important member of the Hayden Survey of the 1860s and 1870s. Lissa has created her own history here as well, founding the Rocky Mountain Ark Wildlife Rehabilitation Center near Telluride, a nonprofit organization that provides a haven for disabled wild animals.

I thought it would be quicker to photograph her mountain lions than to wait for weeks, months, or even years out in the middle of nowhere to get the shots. If you wish, send her a donation or, if you're in the area, drag that deer carcass you saw along the highway up to her place. Her lions are always hungry.

North Halfmoon Creek, Mt. Massive

The water cascades down from far off snow-packed peaks
It gurgles, splashes and laughs along, as if it really speaks
Through forests and valleys it passes by
Bringing life along the way
So enjoy your life to the very best
And live for every day.

A Colorado River

Starting high among the many 14,000-foot mountains of sparkling Colorado, the snow melts into rivulets of bouncing whitewater. These trickles turn into a babbling, crashing water of white. As they join others along the way they grow in size and volume. Many of these streams have become a whitewater mecca for the "river rats" of the world. I began river guiding in 1978 and then joined the ranks and entered into the wild and wet world of kayaking.

So come on along and let me be your guide on an exciting rafting trip on one of the many rivers here in Colorado. First stop, the outfitters shop where you will sign in, change to river clothes, and receive your equipment. This will include a paddle, life jacket, helmet, and spray jacket. Wet suits are readily available if the trip and weather warrant it. One of our guides will give the safety briefing talk and share with all the paddlers how to sit in the raft, different paddle strokes (there are only two: forward or backward), bracing in the raft, and what to do if you do fall out. With snow-melt water, swimming is not something you really want to encourage. Well, the rafts are loaded so let's all hop on the bus and off to the river.

At the put-in the rafts are unloaded and carried down to the river. Food coolers, emergency supplies, a first-aid kit, and extra equipment are loaded. In my raft there are six anxious and excited passengers. They all pile in and I get in last sitting in the back. Everyone is comfortably seated and we are ready to go. With my group I start off with some basic commands. It's quite simple: you either paddle or you just sit.

Now to make it more confusing there are two sides to the raft. A right side and a left. It is quite important to understand what side you are sitting on and to know your left from your right. Please be sure to put the full blade underwater when you paddle. The tip doesn't count and you will definitely hear about it. So that we all stay together as a team, the right front paddler sets the pace. The left front paddles with the right front, and everyone behind follows those in front. "Back paddle everyone," then I quickly call out, "Straight ahead everyone," a pause, "Back paddle left, straight ahead right." The signals continue to get everyone well informed and somewhat comfortable. Not so difficult is it? Well let's try it on fast-moving water with rocks and old trees or other obstacles to maneuver around.

As the countryside passes by, tall canyon walls appear suddenly ahead. That distant roar of thunder is caused by the giant boulders choking the river into a narrower size creating a massive pile of wild and wonderful rapids. Now let's add some rather exciting, winding and twisting drops and you have yourself an adventure beyond imagining. "Back paddle left, straight ahead right! Everyone back paddle! Stop! Straight ahead!" All in about twelve seconds. Waves are crashing, the roar of the rapids is almost deafening, all are soaked, but wait — there is more! Next is "Monster Drop." It's a nine foot drop that looks more like nineteen feet. Oh yes, don't forget to breathe while we are doing all of this. Dropping into a cauldron of boiling and churning whitewater, the raft smashes into a giant boulder. Freddy is "rocketed" into the growling foam; Sherry and Kim bounce to the bottom of the raft.

Quickly I stretch out the T-handle end of my paddle and pull good ol' Freddy back to the side of the raft. I grab his paddle and drop it in the bottom of the raft. You know how it is, a $35 paddle is a $35 paddle. As Freddy is pulled in, the raft is floating sideways into the next drop. "Back paddle right, straight ahead left!" I yell. Freddy is still on the bottom of the raft and someone else is still trying to get back up on his seat. I push Freddy up and out of the way as the raft hits the cascading drop. Everyone is flying arms, legs, and bodies. However, no one falls out as we float into calmer water.

Please take note and enjoy the beautiful canyon scenery. Drift through unusual rock formations, high, sheer canyon walls, various shadings of color on the rocky surfaces, plentiful arrays of summer wildflowers. Oh look, there is a redtailed hawk searching for lunch. In the evening light, deer and other wildlife will make their way down to the river. Right now Freddy is glad that the sun is out and I'm glad that Freddy is out . . . of the river. All are alive and quite happy.

Guess what? It's lunch time. All the rafts gather on a warm sandy beach and we unpack for lunch. It is a great time to take a break and refuel ourselves. Hey, let's wander up a side canyon and explore something unique and exciting. The creek is cold and clear as we wade through it. Around a corner there is a stunning waterfall dropping about thirty feet into an emerald green pool. Shower anyone?

Well, it's time to go back and continue our whitewater journey. As we cruise over the clear flowing water, it seems that we are in a low-flying airplane. As the bottom appears, disappears, and then suddenly reappears we pass over gravel bars and then into deep pools along the way. Then it's more fun-loving rapids, large standing waves that resemble haystacks, narrow chutes and drops. It's a wonderful experience now coming to a close.

The mysterious canyon has melted away to an area of open space and there is a wide sandy beach to end a most adventuresome trip. The bus is there and ready for reboarding. We load the rafts, tie them down and hop back on the bus, perhaps a bit slower this time. The snow-capped mountains that surround us beckon far and beyond. As the bus pulls out I holler, "Everyone back paddle!" There is a roar of laughter and applause as we head west into the afternoon sunlight. Right now, how about a wonderful, hot shower?

San Luis Valley

I looked across the valley wide, the horizon far beyond
It shows there was a magic touch, in the brightness of the sun
Its light so bright it blinded me, but somehow I still saw through
The mystery of an ancient land, and a spirit that was true.
It traveled across the desert, which was deep and wide and long
It guided me by night and day, and I heard its ringing song.
So listen close and don't forget that our Lord is always there
To lift you up and keep you safe, from evil everywhere.

Did you ever watch a sunset turn the ocean into gold?
Did you ever touch a flower as its petals did unfold?
Did you ever wonder why there are rainbows in the sky?
Or how the birds can fly, with just their tiny size?
God knows!

Cactus Flower

Afternoon Thunderstorm

Sunsets

Around the world and across the seven seas there is always a setting sun. It's a wonderful visual masterpiece, always changing. Sunsets are warm, romantic, mysterious, and exciting. Here in Colorado, you can always find a scenic sunset. From the sprawling plains of the east, up through the mountains that dominate the middle of the state, to the wide open spaces of the Western Slope, the sun will set with a different vista. Wherever you are, take the time to watch. There is always that special early evening light as the sun drops lower in the sky. The water vapor and dust in the atmosphere change the light's rays to a warm glow.

It is such a wonderful experience to watch the sky as it turns from a pale reddish pink to a wild, burning red into a deepening shade of purple. And there are never two alike. If there is a rancher driving his stock or ranch equipment across the land, or a dusty road, watch for the wind to stir up the dust. Try to be to the east of the dust for the light to filter through. When there is a haze in the air, watch for the fleeting shadows and silhouettes. When there are high, billowing clouds they are usually the best. As bad as they are, the smoke from forest fires will turn the sky to its own brand of sunset. When you see a warm sunset starting, watch and wait it out. If you have the time, try to get high above the surroundings for a better view.

There are many locations high in the mountains overlooking a far distant valley. During the summer months Trail Ridge Road, Mt. Evans, and Pikes Peak are excellent vantage points. Land's End on Grand Mesa is another. From the high mountain passes to the far ends of the state, just be here. And then there are those rare days when it is totally overcast and snowing. Well, at least we can ski!

The Colorado High Country

Twin Peaks at Twin Lakes

On the Road

Driving through the West conjures up images from old Roy Rogers or Gene Autry movies. Juniper and piñon trees grow among giant boulders. A rise in a hill, or long curve in the road gives way to a sprawling, open valley with grassland reaching to the horizon, and a scattered ranch or two. Over another hill you drop down into a green valley, where a wild, rushing river of whitewater snakes through the valley floor and snow-capped mountains stretch clear up to a deep blue sky. Or you may drive into a tunnel, leaving warmth and sunshine and exit a mile and a half later to zero visibility in a raging snowstorm. That's not too bad if you happen to be going in the opposite direction. Or maybe you drive for miles and miles and see nobody at all.

South Park

Mt. Massive

Clouds and Sky

It's true, the sky does come all the way down to the ground. Where you observe it is what counts. As a kid, I would often watch the big, billowy white clouds slowly gyrate into different forms. I would envision weird animals, scary monsters, and whatever else my mind could conjure up. There were giant creatures, towering snow-white mountains, the list goes on.

Out West the sky does come right down to the ground. When you are out on the rolling prairie, stop and take the time to enjoy what the clouds are offering you. Are the clouds high and wispy? Are they gray and monotoned? Are they big, pillowy white giants that stretch all across the sky? When it is windy, watch the endless wheat fields blowing back and forth like the current and waves on the ocean floor.

One day I was traveling over the plains, when off in the far distance I could see the towering giant clouds rising up and out of sight. At first they were puffy, bright, and white. As I drove closer they grew darker in color until they were almost black. The wind started to blow and the temperature dropped sharply. It was like walking into an air conditioned mall from a steamy hot parking lot.

Then came the rain in torrents. It was so black and windy that driving was reduced to a slow crawl. Lightning flashed, there was a boom of thunder that shook the whole car. It was totally wild. I pulled over and stopped but after a few minutes the sun slowly peeked its way through. Then to the east was a beautiful rainbow. It was most vivid in its colors as it radiated against the black clouds in the late afternoon sun. The road was sparkly and wet with mists of steam as I headed on to somewhere else.

Toponas

Ol' Pete

The valley was deep and wide as we herded the cattle down the trail. It had been long days and short nights of chasing cows, looking for lost calves, and eating cold food most of the time. Now with the coming of autumn, the days were growing shorter and the nights cooling down. The trees had started turning bright gold, pale yellow, rusty red, and parched brown. Some of the high peaks had a velvety dusting of snow. Whistling and swinging our ropes, we kept the herd moving till we got all the cattle into the holding pens. With the last of the cows in, the gates swung closed and a welcome break was at hand. Dusty, tired, and hungry, we washed up and gathered around the chuck wagon for some hot, black coffee and a wonderful dinner of steak, potatoes, and all the scrumptious extras!

Much of the crew hadn't seen one another all summer so it was good to reunite with old friends. I asked where Ol' Pete was and learned that he had been killed in a late spring avalanche up in the high country. I remember Pete from a long time ago. He was originally from Scotland and had a most fascinating accent. He never said much but was right there when a guy needed help. He always seemed to know exactly what to do. He taught me how to rope a cow, mend fences without cutting my fingers all to pieces, and look for strays down in the washes. At night, around the campfire, he'd play his bagpipes and we'd all sit and listen. When I'd be out on night watch on the other side of the herd, I could hear that sweet sounding music echo on and on.

After dinner I walked off through the sage by myself. The cows had all bedded down and were quiet except for a random "moo" here and there. Way off in the distance in a light gentle breeze, I thought I could hear those melodious bagpipes whispering *Amazing Grace.* Ol' Pete was on his last roundup.

One of the enjoyable parts of this project has been traveling and meeting extraordinary people everywhere I go. The weathered ranch hand, the beautiful, dark-eyed Hispanic children, the widowed ranch lady, and the sheepherders. I've met shopkeepers, youngsters, working people, and retired folks from all over, and fascinating folks visiting us from all parts of the globe.

I have listened to their stories of how their parents and grandparents struck out for the frontier, homesteading, ranching, building a store or a town. They survived the elements, economic depressions, accidents, and tragic loss of lives. They shared in the great joy and happiness of watching their fields grow, families being raised, and a new generation growing up.

Here, amid this majestic landscape, with the deep-red sunsets, the towering mountains, the sweeping vastness of the plains, it's the people that give it real meaning. All the beauty in the world can be pretty hollow without someone to share it.

If you have enjoyed this adventure, watch for my next book, *Places and Faces Somewhere Out West*. With this journey I close, and leave you with the thought that there is always hope. All you have to do is add the love. The greatest gift you can give is the gift of love.

Someday

Someday when I grow up, I want to be an astronaut,
  or maybe a cowboy.

Someday when I get big, I want to go to college
  and be a football star.

Someday I want to follow the sun.

Someday I want to climb a great mountain,
  and feel the cold wind blow across my face,
  and stand on the snow-covered summit
  where the air is so clear you can see forever.

Someday I want to paddle down a wild mountain stream,
  crashing and splashing over and around the giant boulders,
  as I journey my way down the river.

Someday I may stumble and fall.

But Someday, I will cross over the Jordan River,
  and reach out and touch the face of God.

The day is done and work has stopped. Ol' Pete has paused to reflect on the days of long ago through the warm, golden rays of a setting sun, somewhere, *Someday in a Place Out West.*